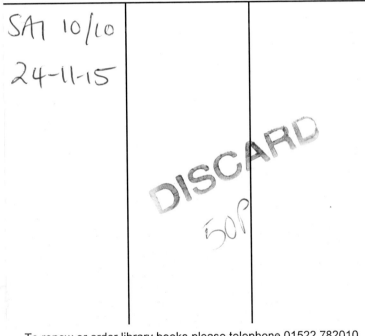

At the
Library

Chris Fairclough and Louise Morrish

WAYLAND

First published in 2008 by Wayland

This paperback edition published and reprinted
in 2010 by Wayland,
a division of Hachette Children's Books,
an Hachette UK Company.
338 Euston Road
London NW1 3BH
www.hachette.co.uk

Managing Editor: Rasha Elsaeed
Editor: Katie Powell
Design: Ruth Cowan
Commissioned photography: Chris Fairclough

British Library Cataloguing in Publication Data:

Fairclough, Chris
At the library. - (Helping hands)
    1. Library employees - Juvenile literature
    I. Title
    020.2'3

ISBN 9780750261722

Printed and bound in China

Acknowledgements
The authors and publisher would like to thank Hampshire
Library & Information Service, and the Library Manager
and staff at Alton Library for their help and participation
in this book.

The website addresses (URLs) included in this book were
valid at the time of going to press. However, because of the
nature of the Internet, it is possible that some addresses may
have changed, or sites may have changed or closed down
since publication. While the author and Publisher regret any
inconvenience this may cause the readers, no responsibility
for any such changes can be accepted by either the author
or the Publisher.

Contents

Words in **bold** can be found in the glossary.

The team

We work at a **public library**. We look after thousands of books, **CDs** and **DVDs** that people can **borrow** and take home. Some people like to stay in the library to read or **surf the net** on a computer.

▼ We are the library team. There are 14 people and a **library manager** in our team.

◀ We work in a busy town library. Up to 600 people visit us every day.

Scanner with date stamp ▼

▼ This is the counter where the books you want to borrow are stamped. It is also where books are returned.

Joining the library

If you want to **borrow** something from the **library**, first of all you have to join as a **member**.

▼ I enter Andrew's name and address on the computer and give him his own library card.

▲ Andrew is a new member at our library. I explain to him how many books he can borrow.

Every new member
to the library is given
a library card. When
someone wants to
borrow something,
they must show the
card at the counter.

▲ Andrew is choosing some books
with his mum.

◀ A library membership card.

I scan the books
Andrew has
chosen. Then I
stamp them
with the date
they have to
come back. ▶

Requesting a book

Librarians and **library assistants** are always on hand to help people out. One of their jobs is to find books for people who **request** them.

▲ I write down the details of the book this customer wants.

◀ I check the computer to see if we have the book. It is not at our **library** so I have ordered it from another library.

Five facts about public libraries:

* The first public library opened in 1851 in Winchester, Hampshire.
* Books used to be chained to the shelves.
* There are 4171 libraries and 655 mobile libraries in the UK.
* 107 million children's books are borrowed every year.
* 660,000 children borrowed 16 million books during the Summer Reading Challenge in 2006.

When the requested book is delivered, I call the customer to tell him he can collect it. ▼

The children's library

The children's **library** is bright and colourful. There are lots of different kinds of books for all ages and interests. The library also has a children's website.

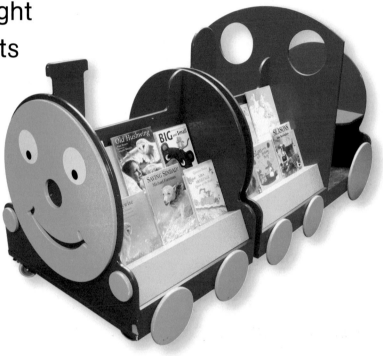

This bookshelf is shaped like a huge toy train. ▶

▼ Will is reading a poetry book about Space with his dad.

Children's Guide to the Library

How do I join?
Ask for a form and fill it in with your parent or carer

Your parent or carer will be asked to show proof of address

Remember, joining is FREE!

What can I borrow?
Up to 8 books. You can choose from:
- ○ Picture books   ○ Story tapes
- ○ Story books   ○ Information books
and they are all FREE to borrow!

And some libraries have videos, music, CD-Roms and DVDs which you can borrow for a small charge.

Hampshire County Council

Storytime for under 5's

Alton Library

10.15am – 10.45am

Tuesday mornings

All children should be accompanied by an adult

Hampshire County Council

▲ Bookmarks tell children all they need to know about our library.

I am choosing
a picture book
to read at
Storytime. ▶

These babies are enjoying Baby Rhymetime. I encourage
them to sing and dance with their mums. ▼

Summer reading challenge

This year's summer reading challenge is called The Big Wild Read. It runs during the summer holidays and all children can join.

Children keep a **record** of what they have read in a special booklet. ▶

Scott is showing me the book he is reading at the moment. ▼

We give colourful stickers to children when they visit. ▼

▲ At the end of the summer, all the readers who have read six books receive a medal.

I give Scott his certificate. He has read a lot of books this summer! ▼

Finding information

As well as books, there are maps, magazines, photographs and old newspapers in the information **library**.

▲ I am helping a caller who is interested in the history of our local area.

Magazines

◀ I look after the magazines and newspapers and make sure they are up to date. People come into the library to read them.

This library has 19 computers that people can use free of charge. Most users come to look for information on the internet.

People can check their **emails**, study and write letters in the library. ▼

CDs and DVDs

Books are free to **borrow** from the **library**, but music and films have a small **hire** charge.

This woman is listening to a music **CD** that she is thinking of borrowing. ▼

▲ She takes the empty CD case to the counter. I find the disk and **issue** the CD to her.

As well as music CDs, the library has
DVDs, videos and computer games
for people to hire. The children's
DVDs are in a section on their own.

I make sure all the DVDs are on the right shelves.
This helps people to find things more easily. ▼

Displays

Some books are very popular. At this **library**, these books are called 'fastbacks'. They are **borrowed** for a shorter time so that more people can read them.

▼ I am displaying some new 'fastback' books by the library entrance. This makes them easy to find.

Sometimes the library holds **exhibitions** and talks.
Local crafts are often displayed for people to buy.

▲ We also sell cards, book bags and notepads. I am arranging some new birthday cards on a stand.

Behind the scenes

The **library manager** looks after the building and makes sure that the **library** runs smoothly. She organises what all the **staff** do. There are a lot of tasks to do every day.

I am the library manager. I am inviting a local school to visit the library. ▶

We are choosing books to buy for the library. We do this every two weeks. ▼

It is important that everything is in the right place in the library so that people can find what they want.

I am making sure these books are shelved in the right order. ▶

◀ When boxes of new books arrive at the library, my job is to unpack and sort them.

Access to all

Many people use the **library** for different things. **Librarians** and **library assistants** will help those who need to use special equipment.

This girl is **partially sighted**. She is writing a letter using a program that makes the text large and clear. ▶

◀ I am helping this customer to use a keyboard that has large keys.

As well as story tapes and **CDs**, there are many **large print** books. The large print makes them easier to read.

▲ I am teaching partially sighted customers how to use the internet.

The library has a hearing loop so that people with hearing aids can hear what is said to them clearly.

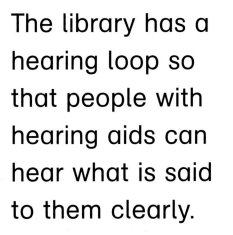
Wide **aisles** make it easier to **access** things and create a feeling of space. ▶

Mobile library service

The mobile library is a big bus full of books, **CDs** and **DVDs**. It goes to villages and estates, where there is no **library** building close by.

The mobile library is very modern. It even has computers that are linked to the internet. ▶

It usually parks in a car park that people can find easily. ▼

It is smaller than a normal library building but there are still lots of books to look at. ▶

You can **borrow** things in exactly the same way, too. ▼

Glossary

access to reach or find something

aisles the spaces in between shelves

borrow to take a book and return it at a later date

CDs compact discs for playing music

DVDs discs for playing films and computer games

emails a message sent from one computer to another

exhibition a display of items

hire to pay money to borrow something

issue to give someone something (a book or CD)

large print where the text has been printed bigger than usual

librarian someone who is trained to work in, or is qualified to run, a library

library a place that contains books, CDs and other material that people can read or borrow

library assistant a member of staff who works at the library

library manager a librarian who looks after the staff who work at the library and the library building

member someone who belongs to a group or organisation

partially sighted when someone cannot see very well

public open to everyone

record to write something down

request to ask for something

scannner a machine that scans information

staff the people who work in a place

surf the net to look at information on the internet

Quiz

Look back through the book to do this quiz.

1 What is every new member of the library given?

2 What can you borrow from the library apart from books?

3 What can people read in the library apart from books?

4 What do children receive when they have completed the summer reading challenge?

5 What is a mobile library?

6 How do librarians and library assistants help people?

7 What do partially sighted people use to help them in the library?

Answers

7 Computers with keyboards that have big keys and large print books.

6 They help people to find out information and to use special equipment.

5 A big bus full of books and CDs that visits places that don't have a library building nearby.

4 A certificate and a medal.

3 Maps, magazines and newspapers.

2 CDs, DVDs, videos, and Computer games.

1 A library membership card.

Useful contacts

www.mrsmad.co.uk
Book reviews, ratings, games, stories, jokes and other useful links for children.

www.askforkids.com
This site can be used for homework help.

www.kidsreview.com
Book reviews written by children.
Includes links to authors' websites.

www.3hants.gov.uk/library/library-children.htm
Look at recommended reads for children and Summer Reading Challenge ideas.

It's great seeing so many children using our library!

Index